Puppy Training Guide for Beginners

How to Train Your Dog or Puppy for Kids and Adults, Following a Step-by-Step Guide: Includes Potty Training, 101 Dog tricks, Eliminate Bad Behavior & Habits, and more.

Lucy Williams

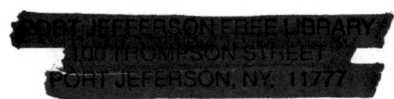

© **Copyright 2020 - All rights reserved.**

The content contained within this book may not be reproduced, duplicated or transmitted without direct written permission from the author or the publisher.

Under no circumstances will any blame or legal responsibility be held against the publisher, or author, for any damages, reparation, or monetary loss due to the information contained within this book, either directly or indirectly.

Legal Notice:
This book is copyright protected. It is only for personal use. You cannot amend, distribute, sell, use, quote or paraphrase any part, or the content within this book, without the consent of the author or publisher.

Disclaimer Notice:
Please note the information contained within this document is for educational and entertainment purposes only. All effort has been executed to present accurate, up to date, reliable, complete information. No warranties of any kind are declared or implied. Readers acknowledge that the author is not engaged in the rendering of legal, financial, medical or professional advice. The content within this book has been derived from various sources. Please consult a licensed professional before attempting any techniques outlined in this book.

By reading this document, the reader agrees that under no circumstances is the author responsible for any losses, direct or indirect, that are incurred as a result of the use of the information contained within this document, including, but not limited to, errors, omissions, or inaccuracies.

Table of Contents

Table of Contents
Introduction
Chapter 1: Puppy Basics

    What Will I Need?
    Puppy-Proofing Your Home
    Bringing Your Puppy Home

        The First Night

    Puppy Development

        Birth to Two Weeks
        Two to Four Weeks
        Three to Twelve Weeks
        Three to Six Months
        Six to Eighteen Months

    Socialization

Chapter 2: Behavior and Training

    Basic Commands

        Sit
        Release
        Stay
        Come
        Heel

    House Training

        Potty Training
        Crate Training

    Walking Your Dog

Chapter 3: Eliminating Bad Behavior and Habits

    Jumping Up
    Biting

Chewing
Barking
Marking

Conclusion

Hey,

Before we start, I want to tell you about an exclusive offer just for readers of this book...

When starting training your dog or puppy, the one thing that you must have is a training checklist to track your four legged best friend's progress. If don't implement this you are setting yourself up for failure before you have even started.

Creating a checklist yourself is super inconvenient, right?

Well yes, it would be, but luckily for you, I have partnered up with Bark Insights. Who are giving away their highly rated dog & puppy training checklist to help you track your pooches' progress seamlessly!

Best thing about this exclusive offer is it 100% FREE, no-strings-attached. Bark Insights usually charge $49 for this exact same checklist to their customers

All you need to do to claim your FREE the training checklist; is type in on your search browsers URL – free.barkinsights.com

Once you are on the web page, fill out the required information that Bark Insights asks for; this should only take less than 1 minute of your time. Then straight away in your email inbox you will receive the checklist that has helped 10,000's of people around the world train their dogs more effectively.

Before reading any further, please do this NOW as I may refer back to the checklist throughout this book!

free.barkinsights.com

Introduction

Are you looking to adopt a puppy for the first time, but don't know where to start or what to do? Or perhaps you have had dogs in the past, and want to make sure that you are teaching your puppy all the right things to be the best that they can be.

People adopt puppies for many reasons. For example, they can improve our health both physically and mentally, they provide us with companionship when we are feeling lonely, and they help us to find out more about ourselves as we learn with them. They can even help you to become more social and meet new people.

No matter what your reason is for wanting a dog, I hope that this guide provides you with all the information that you and your puppy need to succeed.

Welcoming a new puppy or dog into your home can be an exciting time for you and your family. Raising a puppy is an incredible experience that takes time, and it can be filled with love, frustration, and sleepless nights. However, when you put effort into training them and strengthening your relationship with your new best friend, it can be rewarding.

Chapter 1: Puppy Basics

Bringing your new puppy home can be stressful. You might be worried about forgetting something that they need, or you might not know what to expect on their first night home. Below, you will find all the information that you will need to make them comfortable as they adjust to their new home, as well as what to expect as they grow and develop.

What Will I Need?

Before you bring your puppy home for the first time, it is a good idea to prepare and make sure that you have all the items that you might need so that they are able to settle into their new home more easily. This includes:

- **Dog bed.** When you are looking for a dog bed, you should go into the pet store and feel each one. Make sure that the cushion is made of a tough material, but is soft enough for your dog to be comfortable. Many puppies tend to scratch and chew on their bed as they grow, eventually destroying their bed, so you should get a bed that they will not be able to destroy easily. You should also consider how big your puppy is going to get when it is fully grown. For example, if you have a large dog breed, then you should not get them a bed for a small dog breed. You should also get them a blanket or two for when it gets cold.
- **Food.** There are many different options available to you when selecting a brand of dog food. If you are unsure, you can ask your vet for a recommendation. They will be able to help you to choose a trusted brand that will give your puppy all the nutrients that they need throughout their development. However, there might be a chance that your puppy dislikes the brand that you get for them. To avoid this, you can ask your vet for a sample pack, or buy a smaller pack of dog food until you find a brand that they enjoy.

- **Food and water bowls.** When selecting a food and water bowl for your puppy, you should consider how big they are going to get and how much food you will be giving them at each feeding time. For example, if you have a small breed of dog, then you will be giving them smaller amounts of food at each feeding, so you would be able to buy a small sized bowl. If your dog is struggling to reach their food or tipping the bowl over, you might need to consider getting them a different size bowl.
- **Collar and leash.** A collar and leash can be essential in training and socializing your puppy, so it is best to get them used to wearing them as soon as possible. When selecting a collar, I suggest that you choose an adjustable flat collar that is made of a tough material so that it does not get damaged during puppy play time or when they scratch themselves. You should choose a flat leash in the beginning that will give you more control during puppy training. I also suggest getting a harness for your puppy for when you start to walk them, especially if they are a smaller breed of dog. It provides more support, and will not slip off as easily as a collar would. I do not suggest that you use a choke chain on your dog, as this can injure them if they are not used to walking and move around a lot. It can also possibly cause breathing difficulties in some dogs.
- **ID tag.** Puppies love to explore their environment, so it is important for you to get them an ID tag when you get their collar. That way, if they go missing, someone is able to contact you and let you know that your puppy has been found. I suggest getting a smooth metal ID tag with your name and phone number engraved on it if possible. A puppy tends to bite holes into soft plastic ID tags, and it can get damaged and wear off of the disk after a few years of use.

- **Treats.** There are lots of different treats that you can buy for your puppy, from sugar-free peanut butter that you can put inside their toys to lick out, to bacon chews that will keep them busy for a while. When you start training your puppy, you should get a variety of different treats that you can give to them. I find that the best treats you can use during training are soft, small-sized chews, especially while your puppy's teeth are still developing. It is also a good idea to get a few harder chew options for when your puppy starts to teethe, or dental chews that can help to clean their teeth.
- **Toys.** Playing with toys and chews are essential to your puppy's development. It is recommended that you get your dog at least three different types of toys, and try to rotate them every few weeks to keep them stimulated. This way, they won't get bored and turn to destructive behavior. I suggest getting a soft-but-durable toy, a chewy toy, and a rope toy if possible. You can get as many toys as you want, but these are the most common toys that puppies like playing with. Plus, they're usually available in different sizes, depending on the size of your dog.
- **Grooming brush and nail clippers.** While not essential, a grooming brush and nail clippers are good tools to have. It is recommended that you start to use these tools fairly early on in your puppy's development, so that they start to get used to them if you take them to the groomers. If you have a long-haired dog breed, you can run the grooming brush along their coat and get rid of the hairs that they shed. This helps to reduce hair fallout that catches on your bedding and clothes.
- **Dog shampoo.** If you decide to take care of your puppy's grooming on your own, then you will want to get some dog shampoo so that you can give them a bath. Even if you decide to take your dog to the groomers, I suggest that you

get a bottle of shampoo in case there are any accidents in the house or garden, and you need to quickly give your puppy a bath.
- **Crate.** By using a crate, you can provide your puppy with a safe haven that they can escape to as they explore their new surroundings. It is important to take into consideration that your puppy is going to get bigger as they get older, so you need to take care when selecting a crate for them. A crate should be big enough so that you can fit in their dog bed, a newspaper or mat where they can do their business, and their water and food bowls.

Puppy-Proofing Your Home

Before you bring your new puppy home, you should go around the house and pick up any objects off the floors. A puppy learns about their environment by putting items into their mouth. If you feel that anything can be potentially dangerous to your puppy or if there is something that you do not want them to get hold of, put it somewhere that they cannot reach. This can include medicine, sharp objects, cleaning supplies, ant baits, and other poisonous substances.

It is also suggested that you try and keep your puppy in a certain area or room in the house when they are not exploring their new home under your supervision. You should make sure that this area will be easy to clean in case there are any accidents, and that you are not isolating them. By limiting them to this space, they will be less likely to have accidents, and you will have a bit more control over where they are and what they are doing.

To ensure that they stay inside their certain area or room, you can block off their exit by using a barrier, such as a large plank of wood, or by even closing the door or putting up a baby gate if you are keeping them inside the room with you while you are busy.

A barrier that I found was incredibly useful for me while I was training my puppy was a dog pen. Using this barrier, my puppy was able to explore and sniff around in a safe environment where he could eat, sleep, and play, and I did not have to worry about him getting out and being naughty.

Bringing Your Puppy Home

So you have ticked off all of the items that you need and you have decided which area or room that your puppy is going to stay in and installed the necessary barriers. What is next? Well, now it is time to bring your puppy home for the first time!

You will need to consider how you are going to bring your puppy home, and if you should take someone along with you. If you are fetching your puppy and the drive home is long, then you should consider bringing someone along who can sit with the puppy to help them feel more comfortable and soothe them on the journey home.

If your puppy has already been trained to use a crate by a previous owner or the breeder, you can also secure their crate in the backseat and put them inside. This works well if you are alone in the car and unable to bring someone with you on the ride home.

On the car ride home, your puppy might be nervous and restless. You can open the windows or put the aircon on so that the car does not get stuffy and your puppy does not overheat. You should also try not to give them much water on the trip unless you are traveling far.

If you are traveling a long distance with your puppy in the car, then try to bring along a toy or treat for them to chew on, some food and water, a blanket so that they can become comfortable, and their leash and collar for if you stop along the way, so that your puppy can go outside and do their business. Remember to take some poop bags or plastic packets along for picking up their excrements and throwing them away.

If you are worried that your puppy might have an accident, try and take a towel that you are not attached to and some cleaning solutions so that they do not make a mess on your car seats, if there is no way that you can pull over for them.

If you do take someone with you on the trip, then try to have them sit in the back seat where the puppy can have space to move around. Your companion can try and soothe the puppy if they are anxious or restless by placing them in their lap, or holding them and stroking their coat in a calming way.

The First Night

The first day that you bring your puppy home will be filled with exciting new memories as they explore your house and get to know you and your family. However, if you have never raised a dog before, then you might be surprised to find out how little sleep you are going to get for the first few nights until they settle into their new home, away from their birth mother and littermates.

It is suggested that you begin crate training with your puppy as soon as possible. In the evenings when you go to bed, you should put them into their crate next to your own bed with a toy or blanket that has the scent of their mother or littermates on it.

Many people suggest that you can also put a shirt with your scent on it, or a watch underneath your dog bed's cushion. By using a watch, you can imitate the sound of their mother's heartbeat, which helps them to sleep better. You can try a mixture of all of these things and see what works for your puppy to help them relax during the night.

I learned the hard way that letting them sleep in their dog bed without being in a crate meant that I would be woken up to scratching on the side of my bed and lots of mess to clean up in the morning. It is recommended that you do not let your puppy sleep in your bed, because they can develop bad habits and behaviors.

During the first few nights, you will begin to hear your puppy whine or cry out for attention. It is important that you ignore this behavior and do not react to it in any way. If you switch your light on and make a fuss or talk to them, then you will only encourage their behavior and they will continue to do it.

Puppy Development

Puppies develop at a much faster rate than humans do. By four weeks, they can use all of their senses, bark, stand, and walk on their own. Many people believe that for every one year that a dog is alive, it translates to seven years in dog years. So when your puppy turns two, they are essentially 14 years old.

Puppy development is split into five separate stages, from the time that they are born to a few months after they turn one year old. After the puppy development stage they will become an adult, then a mature adult after five years for a large breed dog, and seven years for a small to medium breed dog.

Birth to Two Weeks

From birth to their first two weeks of life, a puppy is unable to hear, smell, or see anything, and will be unable to stand or walk. They are completely reliant on their mother to feed and look after them. During these first two weeks, you will find that a puppy sleeps most of the time. This is important for their growth and development. A puppy will rely heavily on their senses of taste and touch during this time, which they acquire when they are born, to interact with their surroundings.

When a puppy is this young, you will not be able to do much with them. It is suggested by veterinarians that you do not carry them around and handle them too much, because their stomachs can become sensitive and they can begin bleeding internally from overhandling. During this time, you should let the puppy and its littermates be cared for primarily by their mother.

It is recommended that you do not try to be quiet around the puppies, and try to expose them to new sounds and stimulating elements while they are at this stage of development. By doing this, the puppy will be less nervous when introduced to new sounds and experiences when they meet their new families and are taken to their forever homes.

Two to Four Weeks

From two to four weeks, a puppy's eyes will open and their sight, smell, and hearing develops. As these senses are developing, they will become more aware of their environment and begin to stand and walk around clumsily as they get used to their new-found movement. They will also be able to imitate the barks and other sounds that their mother makes and wag their tail.

During this stage, a puppy will begin to interact and socialize with their mother and littermates. This is an important part of the puppy's development because they will learn behaviors from the others, such as weaning and how to eliminate.

A puppy's first teeth will also develop during this time, and from three weeks on you can start to give them more solid food. When you start feeding them solid food, you can put some puppy pellets into a low dish that they won't struggle to eat out of, pour a little bit of boiling water from the kettle over their pellets, and leave it to stand until it has cooled down. This will make the pellets softer for them to eat, and should also make the food smell nicer to encourage them to eat it.

It is now recommended that you try to interact with the puppy so that it gets used to human touch and smells. You should be careful when you handle the puppy so that you do not drop them or injure them unintentionally. In the beginning, you can try and pet or stroke the puppy's coat. If they seem nervous or scared, or if the puppy's mother becomes unhappy with you handling the puppy, then you should not force the interaction.

Three to Twelve Weeks

From three to twelve weeks, the puppy will continue to grow and develop. This stage is the most crucial for them, because they learn how to play and be more social with their littermates. They will also learn to bark and growl. Now is an important time to introduce the puppy to new people and experiences such as vet visits, using the vacuum, or rides in the car.

At five weeks, you can start to house train them. If the puppy's mother is house trained, then they will follow their mother outside when she goes to eliminate and learn to eliminate in the same spots that she does. However, if they do not do this, you can also take them to a designated spot outside and begin potty training them.

At six weeks, you can introduce the puppy to using a collar and lead, and you can teach them to recognize their name and come to you when you call them by it. It is also a good time to begin introducing them to a reward system when they perform desired behaviors by using a clicker, praising them, and giving them treats.

At eight weeks, the puppy can be adopted and go to a new family because it no longer relies as much on its mother as it used to. Once the puppy has received his vaccinations at 12 weeks, he can begin to interact with other dogs and animals, such as cats. It is a good idea to have your puppy interact with as many different types of animals as possible so that they do not become scared or aggressive when they come across them.

From eight weeks old, you can start to house train your puppy, but it is only suggested that you begin with behavioral training at nine weeks and older. Now is a great time for you to plan a training schedule to follow with your puppy.

Three to Six Months

From three to six months, a puppy will experience a big growth spurt and will grow to about the size that they will be when they are fully grown. Their permanent teeth will also start to come out, and they will begin to teethe and chew as they lose their baby teeth.

During this stage, your puppy will identify their rank within their pack, and determine whether they will become dominant or submissive. If your puppy is the only dog in the household, then they will most likely become the dominant dog. If you have many dogs, then they might fight over who becomes the dominant and the submissive.

Your puppy also experiences a period of fear during this time, so it is best to introduce them to as many new situations, people, and other animals as possible and provide them with lots of positive reinforcement. If you are thinking of getting a cat or other animal, now is the perfect time to introduce them into your household so that your puppy does not become scared when they experience these things at a later stage in their life.

You can begin to give your puppy some more independence at this stage. For example, you can give them some free time to relax with you outside of their confined space or crate, and to enjoy a toy or treat. Always make sure that you keep an eye on them and do not let them wander off on their own.

At this stage, you can begin to introduce your puppy to simple behavioral training exercises and commands. When you first start training your puppy, you should train in short intervals of between 10-15 minutes a few times a day, and try to focus on one or two types of exercises at a time.

If you give them too much to do at once, you might end up confusing them. You should only train at the speed that your puppy can handle, or they might not understand and get distracted by other things.

Six to Eighteen Months

From six to 18 months, it is important to continue to socialize, train, and introduce your puppy to new experiences. During this time, your puppy will learn behaviors and habits from their pack. Now is a good time to correct any bad behaviors and habits that your puppy might develop, before they become a problem and are passed on to their pack.

At six months, you can decide if you want to spay or neuter your puppy. There are a lot of health benefits to spaying and neutering, and it can reduce aggression between your puppy and their pack. However, there are some breeds, such as beagles, that can possibly pick up a lot of weight if they are spayed, even if they are following a specific diet. You should speak to your vet before you make this decision for your dog.

During this stage, you can start to teach your puppy more advanced tricks and training. You can also begin professional training with them, such as if they are going to become a show dog or a working dog. You should also get them used to going to the vet on a more regular basis. Provide your puppy with positive reinforcement when you go, so that your puppy is not anxious or scared in the future.

At 12 months old, your puppy should be fully developed and should not continue to grow any further.

Socialization

Puppy socialization is important to the wellbeing and development of your puppy. Socialization is something that should be introduced to them from a young age, and should continue on as they become more mature. You should introduce them to as many new experiences as possible, from meeting people of all ages, other animals, new activities and places to go, and objects around the house such as the vacuum cleaner and hairdryer.

If your puppy is not socialized, they can become aggressive towards people and other animals. When introducing people to your puppy for the first time, you should not have them approach your dog immediately, as this might be overwhelming for your dog and they might bite out of fear. Instead, you should welcome your guests in and have them get settled. Let your puppy come and greet them when they are ready to do so.

Before you introduce your puppy to other animals, you should make sure that they have had their 12 week vaccinations, in case the other animal is unhealthy and bites or injures your dog. To introduce other animals to your puppy for the first time, you should meet on neutral grounds, such as a park, and let them greet and sniff at each other.

Try to remain calm during this meeting, because if you are nervous your puppy might feel this and become nervous as well, and the meeting will not go well. If they are meeting another dog, you can try and take them both on a walk so that they can get used to each other. If this first meeting goes well, then you can continue to take your puppy to meet with the other animal, or you could have a play-date at your house and see how that goes.

If your puppy is not comfortable with the other animal in the house or garden, you might need to continue meeting in a neutral place until your puppy gets used to them.

When introducing a new pet into your household while you already have other pets, you should introduce them slowly, in a certain area in the house or garden where they can see and smell each other. If your other dogs become aggressive or scared, then you should remove the puppy from the situation and try again at another time.

It is important to remember that it can take time to introduce new dogs to other animals, but it should not deter you. You should continue trying to socialize your dog for as long as it takes, while going at the rate at which your puppy is comfortable.

Hey,

As mentioned at the start of this book, you have an exclusive offer available to you for a short period of time.

In case you forgot to claim your 100% FREE, no strings attached dog & puppy training checklist by Bark Insights.

Please can you make sure to do so NOW!

The reason for this is in the next coming chapters I will be discussing and referring back to parts of the checklist that Bark Insights has created for you to improve your dog training experience.

It will be pivotal to have this checklist available at all times as when training your dog or puppy, the training checklist will help you to look back on how far your four legged best friend has come.

In case you forgot how to claim your FREE copy of the checklist, is type in on your search browser URL – free.barkinsights.com

Remember, before reading any further, please do this NOW as I will refer back to parts of the checklist throughout this book!

free.barkinsights.com

Chapter 2: Behavior and Training

Once you have brought your puppy home and they have settled in, it is time to start training them so that they will become the best dog that they can be.

You can start training your dogs in basic behavior and commands from as early as seven to eight weeks old, but it is recommended that you wait until they are nine weeks old before training them to follow commands. Because a puppy cannot focus on one thing for long, it is recommended that you train them in short intervals a few times a day, so that your training sessions are effective.

When you are training, it is important that you remain calm and patient while you teach them in a gentle way, focusing on reinforcing their behavior in a positive way. If they perform the desired behavior, then you should quickly praise them and give them a treat. If your puppy is behaving incorrectly or seems unfocused, then it might be best to stop and revisit your training session again at another time.

You can also incorporate using a clicker that will replace giving your puppy a treat. To do this, hold the clicker in your hand, and when they do the correct command, you must praise them and click the button of the clicker before you reward them with a treat. Once they have become familiar with this, you can slowly decrease the frequency that you reward them with a treat until you only use the clicker instead of a treat.

It is worth mentioning that there are some puppies who do not respond to treats. If this is the case with your puppy, then you will need to use praise or a toy to help them understand that they are performing the desired behavior, and to encourage them to continue doing it.

Basic Commands

When you are teaching your puppy a new command or trick, it is important that you decide on a word that is short and can be said quickly, such as "sit" or "heel". You should only introduce the name of the command once they become familiar with the actions of the command. The name of the command or action that you want them to do needs to be repeated between 50 to 100 times before your puppy can associate the word with the action. It is important that they perform the correct actions before you praise and reward them.

You are welcome to use whichever positive reinforcement technique works for you and your puppy while training them, whether it is a treat, toy, or praise.

Sit

Teaching your puppy to sit is one of the first commands that dog owners teach, and one of the most important. You will begin by standing in front of them. If they seem anxious or unfocused while you are standing, then you can kneel in front of them instead. There are some small dog breeds who prefer this approach, and can become more responsive during your training sessions as a result.

Next, take a treat and hold it above their nose. When they proceed to try to take the treat, move it above their head and backwards as they follow it until they go into a sitting position. As soon as their bum touches the ground, praise them and give them the treat. Continue with these actions until your puppy is familiar with it, then introduce the word "sit" before you hold the treat out to them.

If they do not go into a sit position, gently push their bum to the ground as you hold the treat out to them. However, if they still do not go into the sit position, then you should not force them because you can injure them. Instead, continue to repeat the actions until they become used to the command and understand what you want them to do.

Release

Teaching your puppy the release and stay commands can be essential, especially if they are in a dangerous situation that you need to get them out of quickly. For example, when you walk your puppy, you can use the stay command to stop them from moving so that you can check to see if it is safe to cross the street. Once you have checked, you can use the release command for them to continue following you.

It is recommended that you teach them the release command before the stay command, so that they can better understand the difference between the two commands and what actions you expect them to do. The release and stay commands go hand-in-hand, so you need to make sure that your puppy understands them both.

You can start by standing with your puppy by your side and throwing a treat out in front of them. Once they go forward and take the treat, you must praise them. You should repeat this a few times before you introduce the word "release" before you throw the treat out.

Stay

Once your puppy has learned the release command, you can proceed to teach them the stay command. First, you will use the sit command mentioned earlier to have your puppy sit. When they are sitting, you can turn to face them and give them a treat.

The next time you use this command, pause for a second or two while they are sitting and you are facing them, then give them the treat. Each time you repeat this command, wait a second or two longer than the previous time before giving them the treat.

Once they are able to sit for a while before being rewarded with a treat, then you can introduce the word "stay," after they have gone into the sit position and you have turned to them. If your puppy gets distracted and goes out of the sit position before you give them a treat, then you should reduce the amount of time you are having them wait before giving them the treat.

Once your puppy has learned the sit and stay commands, you can make their training more interesting by using sit, stay, and release in one training session to help your puppy to better understand the use of the commands.

You can also use this command in different situations. For example, when you feed them, you can use the wait command while you fill their food bowl, and then you can use the release command when they can start eating.

Come

To teach your puppy the come command, you will start with taking a treat in your hand and showing it to your puppy. When your puppy approaches you to take the treat, praise them and give it to them. You should continue to repeat this a few more times until your puppy becomes familiar with coming to you when they see the treat.

Next, you will introduce the word "come" as you hold the treat out to them. Once they have gotten used to the command, you can start to move farther away from them and call out the come command with the treat in your hand. When they come to you, you should praise them and give them the treat.

This can be a difficult skill for your puppy to learn. However, if you are patient and continue to practice using the command, your puppy will be more likely to come to you when you call out to them. This can be a crucial skill that your puppy should know, especially if you intend to teach your dog to walk off their leash in public areas.

If your puppy does not come to you or gets distracted when you use the command, you may be training them too fast and will need to either slow down or revisit this training later in the day. When using the command the next time, you should go back to the distance that your puppy was last comfortable with.

Some more advanced exercises that you can use when you are teaching your puppy the come command include:

First, and only once your puppy is comfortable with the command, you can go to another room and call out "come" from that room. When they come to you in the room, you can praise them and give them a treat.

Another exercise you can do is give the members of your family treats, and have each of them call out the come command and give the puppy a treat when they go to them. This is also a great way to help your dog understand that other people can give them commands, and that they should listen to them, too.

Heel

Teaching your puppy to heel can be a handy skill to learn, and will make your life easier when you start to walk your dog. To begin, you will need to put your puppy's collar or harness on and attach their lead. It is suggested that you use a clicker when training a dog to learn the heel command.

You will start by standing with your dog with their lead in your hand, and calling them to your side. You could call them to your left side or to your right side, whichever is preferable to you. Once they move to your preferred side, command them to sit. When they sit, praise them and give them a treat. Continue to repeat this until they are used to the command.

Next, hold a treat in your hand above them and slowly start to walk forward. The treat should guide them as you continue walking. However, if they become distracted or walk ahead of you, then stop completely and call your puppy's name. Once your puppy has returned to your side and refocused on you, then start over with this step.

Once they have gotten used to this, then you can begin to introduce the word "heel." When they follow alongside you, then praise them and either give them a treat or click the button on your clicker. Try and use both of these methods so that they can get used to using a clicker, and so they do not expect to receive a treat each time.

Once your dog is familiar with the heel command, you will notice that taking them for a walk becomes easier, and they will be less likely to walk ahead and pull at their lead. Experts suggest that the martingale collar is the best collar to use when teaching the heel command. This collar provides more support and control over your puppy than a regular flat collar, and is much better for them than using a choke chain.

House Training

When you bring your puppy home for the first time, you should establish where they are going to sleep and where they should relieve themself. House training does not have to be difficult. The speed at which you are able to house train your puppy depends on how attentive you are to training them.

If you only remember to take your puppy outside to relieve themself every now and again when you remember, and if you do not set a schedule and stick to it, then it could take you months to house train your puppy. But if you are attentive and put effort into their training, you can house train them within a few weeks.

Potty Training

Potty training your puppy can sometimes take a lot of time and patience. You might get lucky and be able to potty train without any issues, and that is great. Most of the time, however, you will stand outside for what feels like hours while your puppy is more interested in exploring than doing their business, only for them to have an accident minutes after they go back inside.

By using a crate, you could possibly reduce the time spent potty training, and you will have less accidents in the house. It is important that you choose a crate that is big enough for your puppy to sleep, eat and drink, and do their business in if they need to. This way, if you do not get a chance to take your puppy outside to eliminate, then you at least have a backup plan in place for them.

However, the main purpose of potty training is to teach them to eliminate in the correct place. Whether that is on a pee pad, a newspaper, or outside, the choice is yours. To start potty training, you will need to make a schedule of when to take your puppy outside to eliminate, and stick to it.

If you brought your puppy home between six to eight weeks old, then they will not be able to hold their bladder for long periods of time. Therefore, you should take your puppy outside every hour or two so that they do not have an accident in the wrong place.

To begin potty training your puppy, you should decide on a spot where you want your puppy to eliminate each time. To keep your puppy from wandering outside of that spot and getting distracted by their surroundings, it is suggested that you take them there on their leash.

When you take your puppy to go potty, you must take them to the same spot each time. When they are finished relieving themselves, praise them and give them a treat. While they eliminate, you can decide on a word to use each time when they go, such as "potty," so that they can associate the action with the word.

When your puppy is familiar with the word, you can say it as you take them to their spot. That way, they will understand why they are being taken there and what you expect them to do, if they need to relieve themself.

The best way to start puppy training is to establish a routine with them. You will need to take your puppy out every one to two hours, when they wake up in the morning, before they go to bed, when they have been playing, and after they have eaten and drank water. By establishing this routine, you should be able to fully potty train your puppy in a matter of weeks.

While you are busy working out a potty training routine, you should keep a notebook on hand to make notes of how often your puppy relieves themself and at what time. By seeing how frequently your puppy needs to go potty, you can work out a schedule so that you are taking them to their spot as often as they need to go. These times will change as your puppy gets older.

Crate Training

Crate training is a wonderful way to introduce your puppy to their new home and sleep area, and to avoid accidents while you are busy working out a schedule that works for you and your puppy. Using a crate can provide your puppy with a safe space that they can go to when they want to rest and relax. It can also be an effective house training tool when used correctly.

When you choose a crate for them, it is important that you find one that is large enough to give them the space that they need to sleep, play with their toys, eat their food, drink water, and go to the bathroom if given no other choice.

However, it is important that you do not leave your dog in their crate for so long that they have to relieve themself inside of it. It is not good practice to let your puppy eliminate where they sleep, and could set your potty training schedule back if they continue to do so.

The only time when they should go potty inside of their crate is when it is an accident. When this happens, you should quickly wash and replace any soiled bedding and blankets and lay down a new pee pad or newspaper, so that they are not encouraged by the smell and continue doing it.

You should not keep your puppy inside of their crate for long periods of time. If you have to leave the house and you cannot take your puppy with you, then you should instead look at confining them to an area in the house. However, it is not recommended that you do this often, as it can instill bad habits and behaviors.

A crate should only be used for short periods of time when you are home. You can also use their crate to take them to the vet and to put them inside at night time when you go to bed. Using a crate can help your dog to learn positive behavior and not adopt any bad behaviors, such as chewing on the wrong things, and relieving themself in the house.

At first, your puppy might not be used to being put into a crate, so they may need a bit of coaxing to go inside. You can take some treats and hold it out to your puppy as you lure them inside slowly. Alternatively, you can leave the crate open and let them sniff and smell and go inside on their own the first time, until they are used to it.

You should not keep your puppy inside their crate for longer than about an hour at a time. Every 45 minutes to an hour, you should take them out to relieve themself in their spot, and if they do relieve themself then you must praise them and give them a treat.

There are also other ways that you can reward your puppy when they eliminate outside, such as playing with them, letting them explore and sniff around the house and garden under your supervision, or by taking them for a walk. I suggest that you try and switch up the ways that you reward your dog so that they do not get bored and so that they stay stimulated. After they have been out and about, you can return them to their crate and then let them out again in an hour.

Walking Your Dog

Teaching your puppy how to walk on a leash can be a fun learning experience, and great exercise for both you and your puppy. It is recommended that you do not take your puppy out for a walk in the neighborhood until they have received their 12 week vaccinations, but you can teach them how to walk on a leash in a safe area, such as your garden, until then.

To train your dog to walk on a leash, you should first get them familiar with wearing their collar and leash. What I have noticed that works well is if you put their collar on and connect their leash, and let them run around outside or in an enclosed space for a little while until they get more used to wearing it.

In the beginning, you should not keep the collar and leash on them for too long, but try to do it for about five minutes. Each time you put the collar on them, extend the time by one or two minutes. Once they are able to have their collar on for about 20 minutes and they do not seem bothered by it, then you can continue to let them wear their collar on a more regular basis.

It is important during this time that you associate walking and using their collar and leash to be a happy time for them. To do this, you can give them lots of praise when they have their collar on and make it enjoyable. For example, you can let them chew on one of their toys on the carpet near you while they get used to wearing the collar.

Once your puppy is used to their collar, you will teach your puppy to walk at your side. You can do this by taking a few steps forward with their leash in your hand and holding out a treat in front of them. When they come towards the treat and stand by your side again, then you should praise them and give them the treat.

You can repeat this a few times until your puppy gets the hang of it, and then revisit the training with them again later or the next day. If you try and make walking a daily activity, then your puppy will look forward to it and you can get them ready to go on a daily walk with you.

When your puppy has gotten familiar with catching up with you as you walk forward, then you can make this exercise more interesting by increasing the distance between you and them before you hold the treat out for them to follow after you.

When you are able to take your dog out for a walk for the first time, you should continue to use this exercise until your puppy is walking alongside you. You can use heel commands in conjunction with teaching them to walk if they are familiar with these commands.

If your puppy walks ahead, you should stop and wait for them to return to your side. If they do not want to walk, you might be going too fast, or they may have misunderstood you. You might have to go back and teach them the basics, or take a break and come back to it in your next training session.

Chapter 3: Eliminating Bad Behavior and Habits

Training does not always go the way that we expect it to. If you have never had a puppy before and you brought them home for the first time, you might be unprepared and not know how to properly train them. Or you might have adopted them from a shelter, and their previous owners did not take the time to train them properly. There might also be a miscommunication between you and your puppy, and as a result they develop bad behaviors and habits.

The good news is that there are many ways that we can eliminate a dog's bad behaviors and habits, from jumping up on your guests to digging holes in the garden and marking your furniture. The first step in eliminating these bad behaviors and habits is to understand why your puppy is doing them in the first place. Secondly, it's important to know how you can train them so that you can prevent them from engaging in these behaviors and habits.

Jumping Up

It is common for a dog to learn to jump up. They first learn to do this behavior in greeting, and to get the attention of their mother or a person. If you do not mind that your dog jumps up to greet you when they see you after a long day, then you do not have to worry about correcting their behavior.

However, you should consider the possibility that not everyone will be as accepting of this behavior as you are. You might think that it is sweet, but your guests might find it to be annoying. Your dog might also unintentionally hurt people, or knock them over if someone is not steady on their feet, like if the person is a toddler or child.

To discourage your dog from jumping up, you can start by not acknowledging the behavior and moving out of their reach when they jump up to you. If you give your dog attention in any way when they jump up, they will not understand the difference between negative and positive attention and will continue to do it because it got a response from you.

When you have moved out of the way and your puppy has responded by going back down to all fours, then you can give them a command, such as sit. Once your dog sits, you should praise them and give them your attention or a treat. In this way, you are reinforcing an alternative, positive habit where he gets the attention he is looking for, and will be encouraged to do that instead when he sees you.

Biting

Generally, I have not seen a puppy that is overly aggressive to the point of wanting to bite people and other animals without there being a reason behind it. It is common for a dog to lash out and bite others when they are feeling scared, or if they are territorial and trying to protect their property. Dogs that were previously abused by their owners also tend to show this type of aggression.

A puppy should learn bite inhibition from their mother and littermates in the first few months of their life. As they play with each other, they will understand how hard they are biting and if they are hurting each other. Their mother would typically step in if they are being too rough, show them how to be more gentle, and reprimand them, if needed.

If your puppy is still unsure of their own jaw strength and likes to play rough and bite you, then you can teach them bite inhibition so that they learn to bite more gently, and so that you can prevent them from unknowingly injuring others.

When your puppy was with their littermates, they would give out a yelp whenever they were bitten too hard, and then the other puppy would let go. You should start by using the same method with your puppy. When your puppy becomes too rough and bites, you can say something like "ouch" loudly and firmly. If they continue, then you should get up and stop playing with them until they have calmed down.

Once your puppy understands that they have injured you and that they must bite more gently, then you should teach them the leave it command. To do this, you can hold a treat in your hand and say "leave it." Your puppy might sniff at your hand, but wait until they move away and leave the treat in your hand before praising them and giving them the treat.

Practice this a few times with your puppy. Once they get used to the leave it command, then you can use it when they mouth your hand. When they mouth your hand, say "leave it." When they stop mouthing your hand, praise them and give them a treat. Continue to do this with your puppy until they are familiar with it and no longer bite or mouth.

Chewing

Dogs learn about their environment by putting objects into their mouth. It is normal for dogs to chew on things, and you should not discourage them from doing so. However, when a dog is bored, curious, or anxious, they could potentially destroy objects that they should not have had in the first place.

If you see that your dog is chewing on something that they should not have, you can correct this behavior by making a sound that will distract them from what they are doing, and replace the object with one of their chew toys.

You should not let your dog roam around the house unattended, because they can develop bad behaviors and habits this way. If you are busy with something and cannot watch over your dog, then it is a good idea to put them inside of their crate. If you need to go out, you should confine them to a specific area in the house where they cannot get a hold of things that they should not have.

Barking

Dogs bark to communicate and alert people and other animals to what is going on around them. There are some dog breeds, like chihuahuas, who are more vocal than other breeds. However, if they are trained properly and get enough exercise and stimulation in their lives, then you should not have to worry about them excessively barking, and you have to correct this behavior.

Sometimes, when animals are anxious, bored, or seeking the attention of others, they will begin to bark excessively. This can become a problem for your neighbors and visitors if you do not try to correct the behavior with your dog.

Dogs guard their home, and most of the time they will bark to warn you of a person walking past your house or trying to break into your home. It is not suggested that you punish your dog for barking, but instead should go and see what they are barking at.

You should allow your dog to continue to alert you to these occurrences without them being worried that you will punish them or react negatively. However, if your dog is barking excessively at a pigeon or something else that is unimportant, you can teach them the quiet and speak commands. It is suggested that you teach them these commands separately so that they do not get confused.

To teach the quiet command, you must put your dog into a situation where they will bark, such as someone knocking on the front door. When they are barking, you should go and take a look at what made the noise, and then return to your dog and try to get their attention. Once they have stopped barking, you should praise them and give them a treat.

You should repeat this process continuously. Once they are used to it, you can begin to introduce the word "quiet". To make this more challenging, you can have your dog wait a second or two longer before you reward them with a treat. Once your dog is familiar with the quiet command, you can give the command whenever your dog barks and you have checked what they are barking at.

To teach your dog the speak command, you should also try to put your dog into a situation where they will bark, like with the quiet command. Once your dog barks, you should praise your dog and give them a treat. Once they are used to this, you can introduce the word "speak," until they are familiar with the command.

Once your dog has mastered the quiet and speak commands, you can use them together so that your dog can understand when they should be quiet, and when they should bark.

Marking

Dogs like to leave their scent on objects outside and around the house. Sometimes they like to have multiple places around the garden or house that they mark frequently, such as against a tree or post, against the legs of chairs, against a dustbin, and even against curtains.

Marking most commonly occurs with male dogs, but females have been known to partake in this behavior as well. Dogs tend to do this when they are left unattended in the house, and use it as a way to display to other dogs and animals that those areas are their territory.

I often see this behavior in dogs where there are multiple males or females in the household, so that they feel the need to display their dominance to the others in the group. Dogs who are the only animal in the household do not tend to do this, unless they are nervous or anxious.

It is suggested by veterinarians that if you neuter your male dog or spay your female dog, they are less likely to mark their territory. However, this does not always work well, unless you do this at the recommended puppy age, before they get into the habit of marking.

If your pet has already started marking, it will be more difficult to get them to stop even after they are neutered or spayed. Still, it is not impossible. Spaying and neutering your pet does reduce the frequency that they mark, so it can be a great place to start when you are trying to correct their bad habit.

To correct marking behavior, you should start by not letting them roam around the house unattended, and should instead confine them to an area of the house or to their crate if you are unable to keep an eye on them.

Next, if you see them marking an object inside of the house, you should make a loud noise, such as clapping, to get their attention.

Once you have gotten their attention, you can take them to their potty spot and wait for them to do their business. Once they have relieved themselves, then you can reward them with praise and a treat.

Once your puppy has done their business outside, you should remove the soiled objects immediately and wash them or wipe them down. You can also use a deterrent spray on the items that your dog frequently eliminates on.

Conclusion

As your dog gets older, they will become calmer and start to settle into their life with you. You should continue to train them and practice commands and tricks to keep them stimulated and alert. It is not true what people say: old dogs can definitely learn new tricks. The secret to lasting results and a happy dog is to provide them with life-long learning and training.

When you put the time and dedication into training your dog, your bond with them will become stronger, and they will become a better companion to have in your life. Through training, you can enjoy the lasting results that this brings, and not spend so much time on trying to eliminate their bad behaviors and habits, or having to confine them to an area when you invite guests over.

Some benefits of obedience training are that your dog becomes more social and friendly with people and other animals, and will not become aggressive and unintentionally injure those around them. They will also be able to provide you with a level of safety and security if taught the bark and quiet commands, and they can even help you to become more active socially with your friends and neighbors.

It is important that you have other people, such as your family and close friends, also practice training and teaching new skills to your dog, so that they do not get used to only receiving commands and training from you. This will help your dog to become more well-rounded and controllable in situations that you might not be able to predict.

If You Enjoyed This Book In Anyway, An Honest Review Is Always Appreciated!

Hey,

Firstly thanks for completing my book this should set you up for success by putting you on the right path.

Remember, there are particular tools that you need not just to make training your dog easier, but make it more effective.

The first crucial tool you will need to make sure you have, so you do not fail, is the dog & puppy training checklist by Bark Insights.

As when starting your pooches training journey, the one thing that anybody who reaches success has; is a detailed checklist to track the progress you have made.

To create a detailed plan to have a mindset shift that you'll need to set you up for success; you have to do endless amounts of research to get mental clarity, acquire new daily habits, and much more.

Creating a checklist yourself is super inconvenient, right?

Well yes, it would be, but luckily for you, I have partnered up with Bark Insights. Who are giving away their highly rated dog & puppy training checklist to help you track your pooches' progress seamlessly!

Best thing about this exclusive offer is it 100% FREE, no-strings-attached. Bark Insights usually charge $49 for this exact same checklist to their customers

All you need to do to claim your FREE the training checklist; is type in on your search browsers URL – free.barkinsights.com

Good luck on your journey and enjoy the checklist!

free.barkinsights.com